Do You See What I See?

A story about Christmas

Written by **Natasha Powell**
Illustrated by **Nadia Ronquillo**

Do You See What I See? A Christmas Story
Copyright© 2024 by Natasha Powell

Written by Natasha Powell
Illustrated by Nadia Ronquillo
Special thanks to Nikki Deaton & Annette Szafranski

All rights reserved. No part of this publication may be reproduced, stored in retrieval system or transmitted in any form by any means electronic, mechanical, photocopy, or recording in any form without prior permission of the author, Natasha Powell.

All Scripture referenced from the New King James Version Bible, New Living Translation Bible, or New American Standard Bible.

ISBN: 979-8-218-53948-1

For Him and for the children.

Matthew 19:14 —

"Let the little children come to Me…"

I love Christmas time! Don't you?
So much to see, so much to do.
People sharing holiday cheer.
It's my favorite time of year!

Everyone likes decorations, no doubt,
And some remind us what it's all about.
If we look closely, then we will see
Jesus in Christmas – I'll show you what I mean.

Do you see what I see?
A star on top a Christmas tree,
With sparkling lights winding down,
Leading to where gifts are found.

Can you find 5 stars in this picture?

What's that have to do with Jesus, you say?
Turn the page quickly. Don't delay.
We'll read what the Bible records of starlight.
Then will you know? I think you might.

Some wisemen from the east came from afar.
To worship the Savior, they followed a star.
The star shone brightly to show them the way
To Bethlehem where baby Jesus lay.
(Matthew 2:1-10)

Now when you see a tree with a star up high,
You'll remember this story and know why.
At the first Christmas, starlight played a big role
To help people find Jesus – Let's make that our goal.

Fun Time Follow-up:
Listen to the Christmas carol, "We Three Kings."
It's about a star! You can act it out and sing.

Have you ever seen angels on a Christmas card?
Or maybe you've seen one in your neighbor's yard.
Some even put one on top of their tree
Instead of a star - now why would that be?

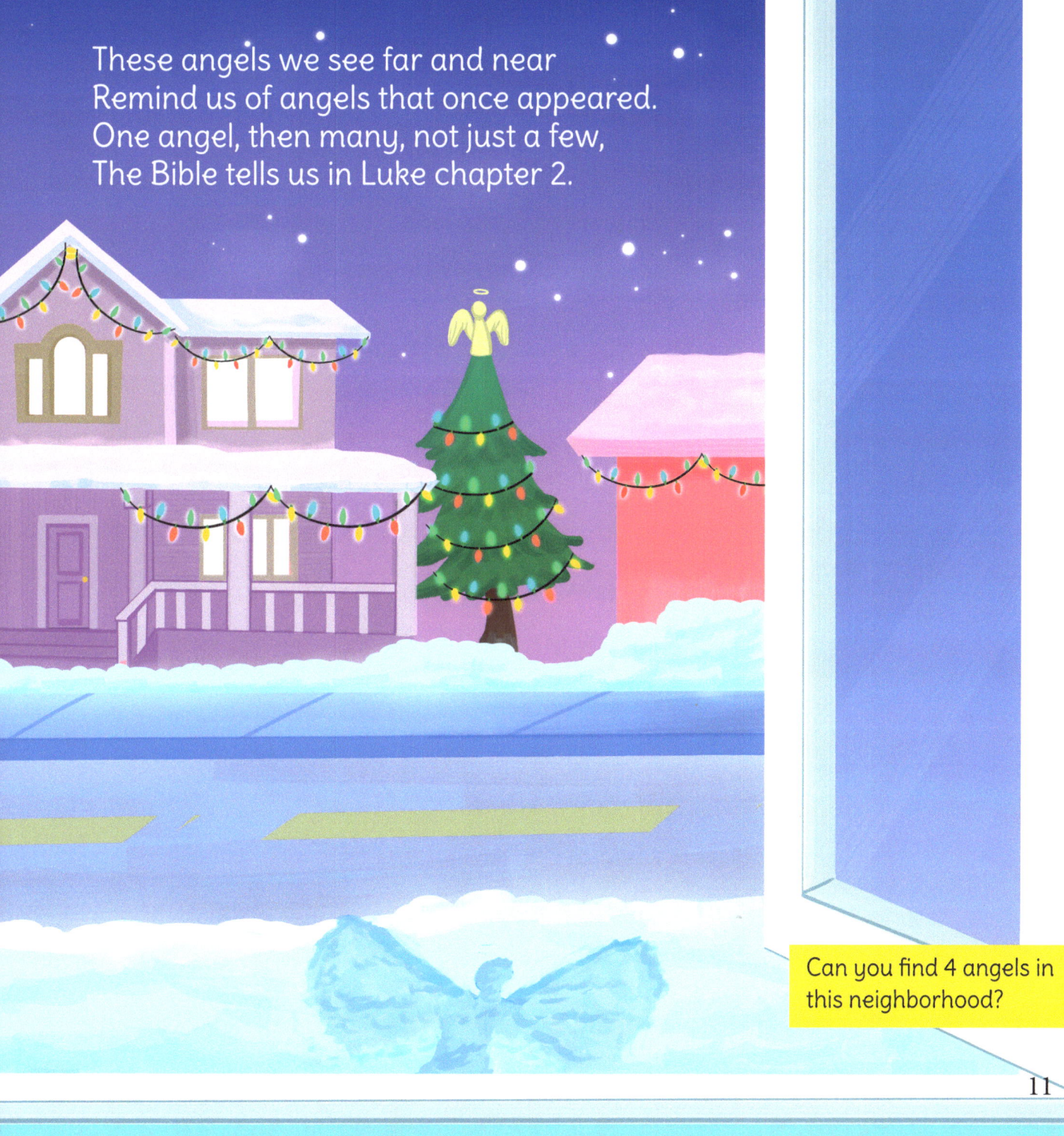

These angels we see far and near
Remind us of angels that once appeared.
One angel, then many, not just a few,
The Bible tells us in Luke chapter 2.

Can you find 4 angels in this neighborhood?

In fields nearby, shepherds watched lambs and ewes
When angels appeared to give them good news.
"The Savior is born. It's the day of His birth!
Glory to God and peace on earth!"
(Luke 2:8-14)

One angel said, "Don't be afraid."
Then told them where the baby was laid -
In Bethlehem, in a manger there,
To bring joy to people everywhere.

Fun Time Follow-up:
Listen to "Hark the Herald Angels Sing."
Oh, what fun Christmas songs can bring!

It's always fun to visit a store.
Goodies piled high - no room for more.
Shelf after shelf of dolls, games, and toys!
So many options for girls and boys.

Can you find 3 wrapped gifts in this store?

After shopping in town, we wrap our gifts.
They're all for December 25th.
But why are presents part of this day?
Let's see what the Bible has to say.

The wisemen arrived at the house with much joy.
They bowed down to honor this little boy.
In the city of David, just like they were told,
They worshiped with gifts of myrrh, frankincense, and gold.
(Matthew 2:11)

Now do you see why gifts are a part?
Presents were given right from the start.
But the very best gift that's ever been given
Is Jesus, God's Son - He makes our lives worth livin'.

Fun Time Follow-up:
"O Come All Ye Faithful" must be heard.
Maybe you'll sing as well as a bird.

Remember the shepherds? They said, "Let's go see!"
And found Mary and Joseph with the baby.
God's precious gift was, as the angels said,
Lying snuggled in a manger bed.

The shepherds went out and told everyone
What the angels had said about this small Son.
All who heard it were simply amazed,
Then the shepherds returned giving God all their praise.
(Luke 2:15-20)

Fun Time Follow-up:
Listen to "Do You Hear What I Hear?"
This song will bring some Christmas cheer.

Brooklyn's

This candy cane came from a bakery stand.
It looks like a shepherd's staff in my hand.
Shepherds weren't popular, some would say,
But God chose to use them in a special way.

Bakery

Can you find 6 candy canes in this picture?

He trusted the shepherds to spread the good news.
Now we can be trusted to do that, too.
Let's turn the candy cane to the shape of a J.
J is for Jesus! Let's tell others, ok?

Here is a farm with much to explore,
And do you see the wreaths on the door?
The wreaths are used to welcome our friends
Because circles are symbols of love with no end.

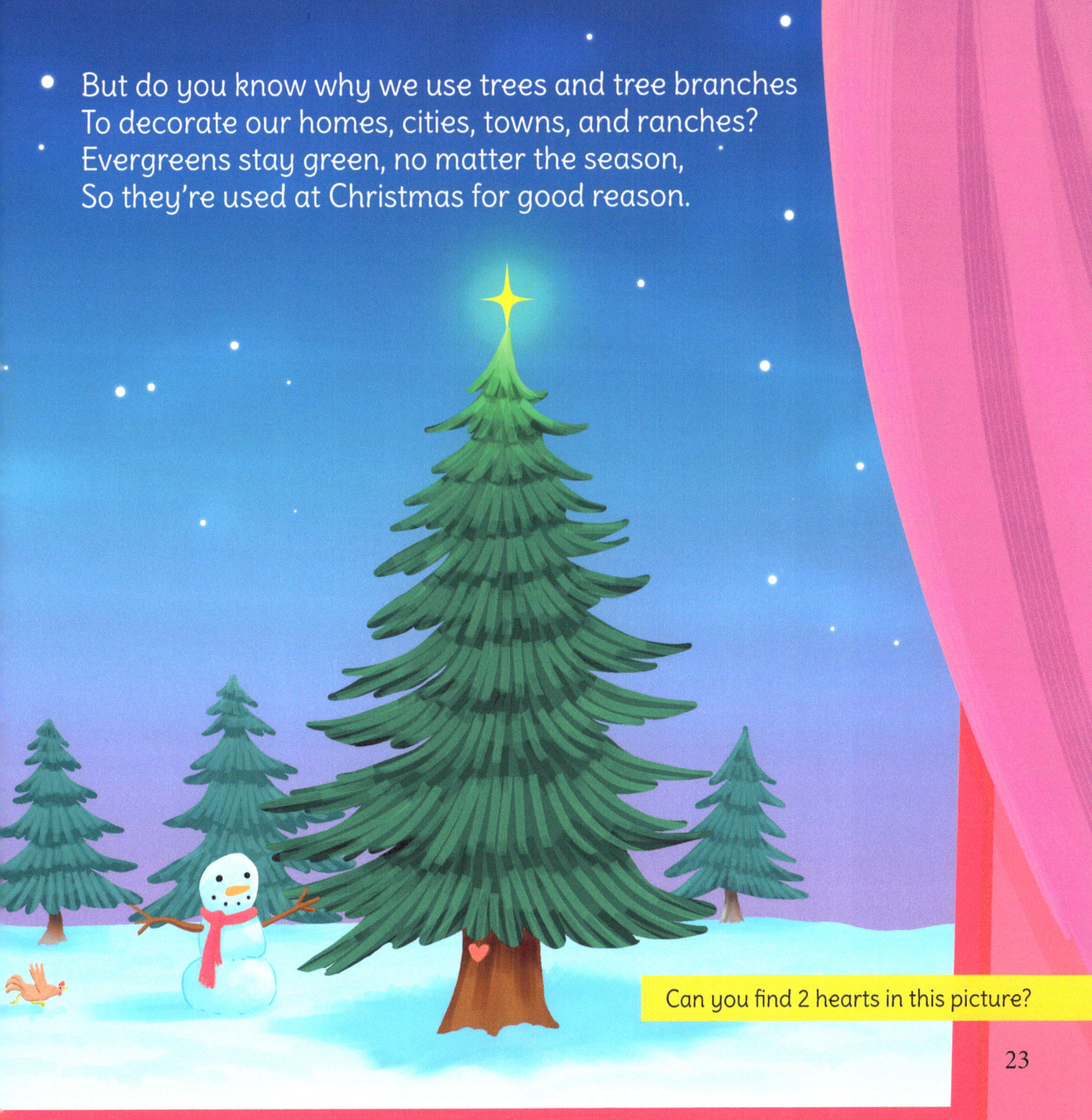

But do you know why we use trees and tree branches
To decorate our homes, cities, towns, and ranches?
Evergreens stay green, no matter the season,
So they're used at Christmas for good reason.

Can you find 2 hearts in this picture?

An evergreen represents life evermore,
And that's what Jesus came to earth to restore.
Everlasting life filled with peace, love, and joy
Such a big mission for so small a boy.
(John 3:16)

The angel called Him Jesus, God's only Son.
The shepherds said Savior, the Christ, Chosen One.
The wisemen had mentioned He'd someday be King.
And Mary, she loved Him and treasured these things.
(Luke 1:30-32, Luke 2:11,17,19, Matthew 2:2)

Fun Time Follow-up:
Listen to "Joy to the World" to brighten your days.
Let heaven and earth ring out His praise!

So, when I see lights that fill up a tree,
I think of Jesus and how great it would be
To spread His light through the world to all –
To old ones, young ones, short and tall.

Fun Time Follow-Up:
"Go Tell It On The Mountain" should be sung.
Sing it boldly; use those lungs!

In the lights, in the gifts, in the songs we sing,
I can see Jesus in everything!
I'm just so thankful for all He's done.
He's on my mind, and I love Him a ton!

Would you consider loving Him, too?
That's the only gift He'd want – it's true.
Then maybe, just maybe, you'll be reminded like me
To look at Christmas and see what I see.

If you love Jesus and want to make Him your Savior,
pray this prayer with me:

Jesus, I love you.
I accept you as my Lord and Savior.
Please come into my life
and lead me.
I will trust You.

Amen.

What's your favorite part of Christmas?

Natasha Powell (author) lives in Michigan, USA. She loves spending time with her husband David and daughter Brooklyn. Natasha enjoys reading books, learning fun new things, teaching and helping others. She wants children to know God and His Word so they will be strong and do great things.
 Find out more at JustLikeJesusKids.com.

Nadia Ronquillo (illustrator) Nadia Ronquillo is a children's book illustrator, visual development artist, and content creator from Ecuador. She majored in Graphic Design and Audiovisual Production. Right away, she started freelancing as a children's book illustrator and collaborating remotely as a visual development artist. For projects, please visit her website at www.nadiaronquilloart.com.